BALLS!

by
Michael J. Rosen
Illustrations by John Margeson

DARBY CREEK PUBLISHING

Text copyright © 2006 by Michael J. Rosen

Cover illustrations by John Margeson © 2006 by Darby Creek Publishing

Cataloging-in-Publication

Rosen, Michael J., 1954-
Balls! / by Michael J. Rosen ; illustrations by John Margeson.
    p. ; cm.
ISBN-13: 978-1-58196-030-3
ISBN-10: 1-58196-030-1
Includes bibliographical references (p.).—Summary: Learn about the balls used in basketball, soccer, football, tennis, handball, golf, volleyball, and ping pong: how they're made, why they look the way they do, some amazing facts about their history . . . and a bit about the games that use them, too.
1. Balls (Sporting goods)—Juvenile literature. 2. Ball games—Juvenile literature. [1. Balls (Sporting goods) 2. Ball games.] I. Title. II. Author. III. Ill.
GV749.B34 R674 2006
[796.3] dc22
OCLC: 60934421

Published by Darby Creek Publishing
7858 Industrial Parkway
Plain City, OH 43064
www.darbycreekpublishing.com

Printed in the United States of America

2 3 4 5 6 7 8 9 10

Ball Basics
Let's Get the Ball Rolling!

The wide, wondrous world of balls includes every sort of orb and globe and sphere that you can think of—including, of course, the world itself! From planets to subatomic particles, from meatballs to ball bearings, the sphere is simply one of the most natural shapes in the universe. If gravity had a favorite shape, it would be the sphere, with its exceptional ability to spin, rotate, balance, store energy, and hold helium so it can float away at birthday parties. A ball just rocks, no matter *what* it's made of!

The world of balls can be divided in many ways.

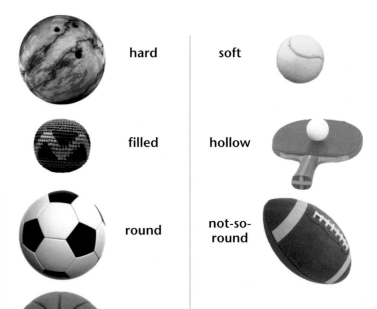

	hard	soft	
	filled	hollow	
	round	not-so-round	
	bigger than a breadbox*	smaller than one	

*And while we're on the subject, has anybody seen a breadbox lately?

ROUNDUP

You'll discover that some of our best-known sports balls have had a few makeovers during their lives, shrinking or growing, gaining or losing weight, wearing more or fewer wrappings, changing their colors and/or composition. Some balls have even gone vegetarian, giving up animal products (cow leather and pig bladders) for a more synthetic lifestyle (rubber and plastics).

Another way to see the spectrum of balls is by what we do with each ball once it's in the game:

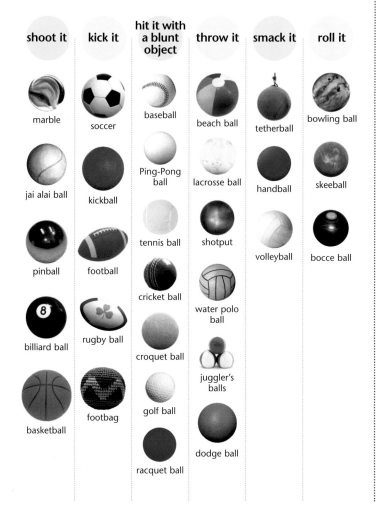

shoot it	kick it	hit it with a blunt object	throw it	smack it	roll it
marble	soccer	baseball	beach ball	tetherball	bowling ball
jai alai ball	kickball	Ping-Pong ball	lacrosse ball	handball	skeeball
pinball	football	tennis ball	shotput	volleyball	bocce ball
billiard ball	rugby ball	cricket ball	water polo ball		
basketball	footbag	croquet ball	juggler's balls		
		golf ball	dodge ball		
		racquet ball			

WINNER AND STILL CHAMPION!

Before we take this big world of balls and start it spinning like a basketball on your finger, let's ask one more question: Why haven't humans created athletic games that use squares, pyramids, or some other shapes rather than spheres? Imagine the wonders of the basketball cube: hard to dribble, nearly impossible to fit into the round basket, but really easy to stack up in the gym supply closet! Or how about a five-pointed soccer ball? Fans might love seeing shooting stars across the field, but players would probably start seeing stars after heading the ball a few times. Cylindrical golf balls? Heart-shaped tennis balls? Forget 'em! Whether hard or soft, large or small, perfectly round or slightly oval, there's nothing like a sphere when it comes to sports. So what are we waiting for? Let's play ball!

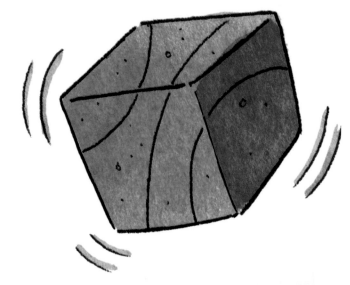

What dribbles but isn't wet, banks but isn't rich, and swishes but isn't a fish?

The Basketball!

Careful where you dribble!

ACTUAL SIZE!

THE INSIDE SCOOP

8 panels of orange leather
cover the ball. All NBA balls are made of leather or composite or synthetic leathers or rubber (for outdoor surfaces). The WBNA uses a ball with alternating panels of orange and white.

Shallow glued seams
(also called ribs) are no more than 1/4-inch deep.

The weight
is between 20 and 22 ounces. (Some leagues for women and youth specify slightly lighter balls.)

Inflated bladder
holds pressurized air of between 7 1/2 and 8 1/2 pounds per square inch.

9" diameter
(The rim on the net is 18 inches in diameter—so two balls, touching, can just fit inside a rim.)

What's a Ping★Pong Ball Doing in Basketball?

Instead of using basketballs, the NBA numbers fourteen table tennis balls from 1 to 14 to determine the order for drafting players. The balls are placed in a drum and are pulled out four at a time, which makes 1,001 possible combinations. Each combination is assigned to an NBA team, and luck of the draw determines which teams are the first to choose new players.

air ball: a ball you shoot that makes you say "shoot," because it missed not only the net, but the rim and the backboard, too.

brick: another bad shot in which the ball is too low and bounces hard off the backboard or the rim—like a brick thrown against a wall.

buzzer beater: a ball that flies through the basket just as the buzzer signals "time's up!"

swish: a ball that drops straight through the net without touching the rim or backboard— the sound of the sweetest shot in the game.

BOUNCE  ABILITY

A ball must be inflated so that when it's dropped from a height of 6 feet, it will bounce about 70% of the way back (between 49 and 54 inches). Official heights depend on which league you're playing in. The key factor for a basketball is how it handles. Players need a ball that's easy to grip, but doesn't stick when it's being thrown and doesn't lose air pressure. Spalding has a basketball with a built-in pump. When the ball's feeling a little squishy, you release the pump, add a few pounds of pressure, and push the pump back inside the ball. What will they think of next? Basketballs filled with sports drinks and built-in straws?

QUESTION A BALL

If my friend is six inches taller than I am, and we both hold basketballs over our heads and then drop them, will my friend's basketball bounce higher than mine?

Answer: As a ball falls, it gathers kinetic energy. Think of that as the fuel of possibility! It's like winding a spring. When the ball hits the ground, all the energy it gathered on the way down is ready to be released. The higher the drop, the more energy is stored up for the rebound. Hard, bouncy balls (like a SuperBall) don't lose very much energy when they hit the floor, so they use the stored energy to spring up high. Squishier balls, like basketballs, lose some of that kinetic energy when they flatten as they hit the ground, so they don't bounce back as high. So your taller friend's ball, since its piggy bank of energy is fuller, will bounce higher, even though the difference will be small.

What's black and white and sometimes red all over if you accidentally stop it with your face?

LOOK!

The Soccer Ball!

(Look, Ma! No hands!)

ACTUAL SIZE!

occer has more fans around the globe than basketball, baseball, and football put together. An unbelievable 33 billion people worldwide tuned in to the games of the 2004 World Cup! And no wonder—this "kick" of a sport has been around for 3,000 years. The perfectly natural action of kicking around a round object has origins in many countries. Ancient China and Japan played soccer-like games with a leather ball stuffed with hair. (Not the same thing as your kitty's hairball.)

The Greeks and Romans played a few ball games, too, such as *episkyros* and *harpastum*, that involved pronouncing those strange words and kicking a smaller, harder ball. Early Olympic games in Rome included such fierce competitions that two-thirds of a team's 27 players often needed medical attention after a 50-minute match. (And this is centuries before Band-Aids, dissolvable stitches, and "I was a great patient" stickers.)

Early South American cultures devised games in which the ball symbolized the sun and had to be "conquered" in the game, ensuring a great harvest. They also created other games that symbolized battles between the gods of the heavens and the lords of the underworld. Mayans and Aztecs played versions of *ulama*, a life-and-death game in which the head of a player from the losing side of the last game was wrapped in rubber and became the ball in the next game. Talk about really sore losers! Makes you wonder if this is where the idea of "heading the ball" came from. Or maybe it doesn't . . .

Harpastum was a rugby-style game (you could use your hands and feet) and was used by Julius Caesar and his generals as a form of military training to improve the physical fitness of the Roman army.

Today's soccer game evolved from various types of "mob football" played in England. Finally, in 1863, players of several teams had a conference to establish the first real rules. Players disagreed on three main topics: tripping, shin kicking, and carrying the ball. The guys who wanted to banish those three activities from the game created soccer (which everyone in the world, except Americans, calls "football"). The other guys who didn't want to give up the tripping, shin kicking, and carrying of the ball made their own game, rugby, which comes closer to what Americans call football. It also comes with more grass stains and bandaged shins.

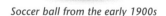

Soccer ball from the early 1900s

THE INSIDE SCOOP

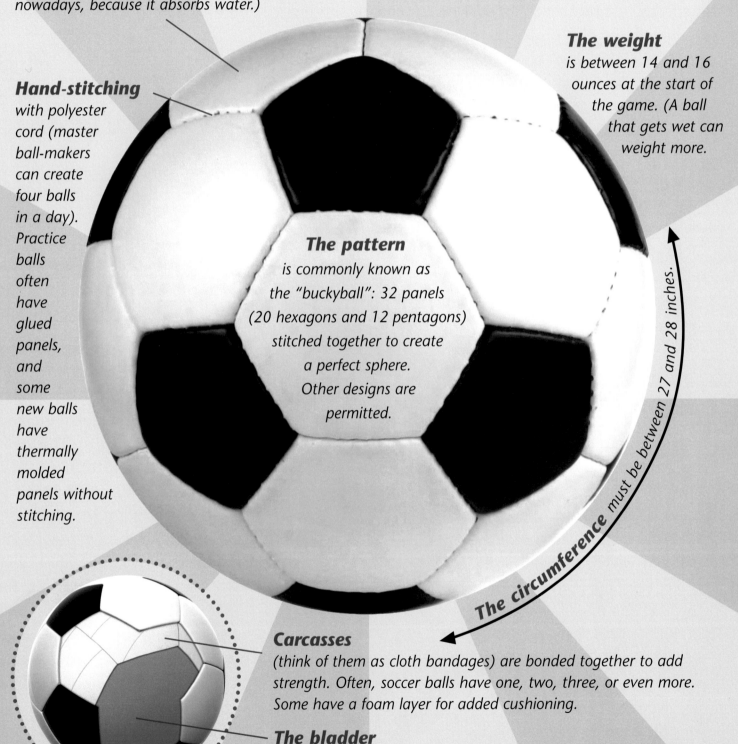

The cover
is a sphere of synthetic leather or other acceptable material in panels. (Full-grain leather is rarely used nowadays, because it absorbs water.)

Hand-stitching
with polyester cord (master ball-makers can create four balls in a day). Practice balls often have glued panels, and some new balls have thermally molded panels without stitching.

The weight
is between 14 and 16 ounces at the start of the game. (A ball that gets wet can weight more.

The pattern
is commonly known as the "buckyball": 32 panels (20 hexagons and 12 pentagons) stitched together to create a perfect sphere. Other designs are permitted.

The circumference must be between 27 and 28 inches.

Carcasses
(think of them as cloth bandages) are bonded together to add strength. Often, soccer balls have one, two, three, or even more. Some have a foam layer for added cushioning.

The bladder
is made of latex, butyl, or synthetic material with air inside pressurized to 8.5 to 15.6 pounds per square inch.

BALL of FAME

For whatever reason, soccer balls seem to inspire people to do crazy things. They just can't seem to put the ball down.

Playing Footsie

Who: Abraham Munoz of the United States
Event: He holds the longest time balancing a soccer ball on one foot.
Record: He kept toe-tapping the ball for 13 1/2 minutes.

Bigfoot

Who: Robert Smith of the United Kingdom
Event: He kicked a soccer ball the farthest.
Record: In 1974 he set the record, sending a ball a distance of 212 feet.

Head's Up!

Who: Adalberto Sanchez of Mexico
Event: He spent the longest time balancing a ball on one's head.
Record: He balanced the ball in place for 2 hours (without a flat-top haircut)!

A★Head of the Game

Who: Agim Agushi of Kosovo
Event: He walked the greatest distance while heading a soccer ball
Record: In 2002, Agim walked 9 miles and 857 yards in 3 hours and 12 minutes.
What's So Great: Two years later Mr. Agushi also headed the ball for a mere 4 1/3 miles—while driving! (The top was down on the convertible, of course.)

The Reign of the Soccer Ball

The soccer ball itself has evolved in several key ways. Here's a time line that shows the big improvements.

Middle Ages, England

(from about 500 A.D. to 1500 A.D.)
For centuries, various balls are kicked (as are the opposing players) in village-against-village competitions. Teams of all sizes play on streets, across streams, and in town squares. Several kings outlaw football and lock up players in jails. The game disturbs the peace, damages property, and mangles players and spectators alike.

Team Handball

Played in 140 countries, team handball is a cross between soccer (players score by tossing a ball into a net guarded by a goalkeeper) and basketball (there's dribbling, free throw shots, and a court that's slightly larger than a basketball court). Two seven-member teams can use any part of the body to catch, stop, or throw the ball, but players can only hold a ball in their hands for three seconds.

About the size of a cantaloupe, the leather ball in this game has a circumference of 23 to 24 inches and weighs between 12 and 14 ounces. Teams of youth and women use lighter, smaller balls. A point is scored when a player lands a ball between the opposing team's goal posts.

1855-1863

Using sulfur, heat, and pressure, rubber is vulcanized! Whoopee! Now soccer balls can be molded into more uniform shapes thanks to Charles Goodyear (yep, the tire guy)! This ball was used in the 1863 match between the Oneida Football Club and the team from Boston High and Boston Latin Schools.

1900s

With stronger rubber inner tubes and tanned leather covers (made up of 18 sections and 3 strips), the balls are stitched inside out, and then reversed. A bladder is slipped in, the cover is stitched shut, and the ball is inflated. Easy to kick, these balls get very heavy when it rains.

BALL TALK

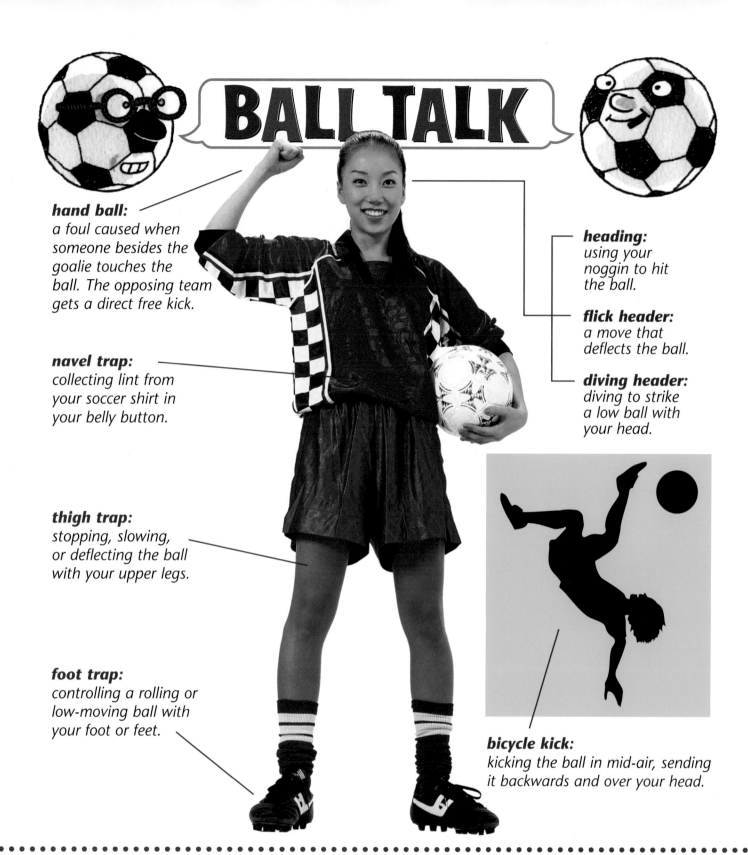

hand ball:
a foul caused when someone besides the goalie touches the ball. The opposing team gets a direct free kick.

navel trap:
collecting lint from your soccer shirt in your belly button.

thigh trap:
stopping, slowing, or deflecting the ball with your upper legs.

foot trap:
controlling a rolling or low-moving ball with your foot or feet.

heading:
using your noggin to hit the ball.

flick header:
a move that deflects the ball.

diving header:
diving to strike a low ball with your head.

bicycle kick:
kicking the ball in mid-air, sending it backwards and over your head.

1940s

An inner layer of strong cloth is added between the inner tube and the leather cover. The invention of a new valve means no need for laces on the ball.

So what happens to all those spools of unused lacing material? Lanyards for lifeguard whistles are born! And counselors have something new for craft time at camp!

1950s

White balls (for night-time play) and orange balls (for snowy playing fields) help spectators and players follow the game. This is true! (And 50 years later, a glow-in-the-dark soccer ball found its way onto the nighttime field, although it has never gone pro.)

1960s

The first synthetic materials replace the leather covering. For the first time, balls have a more predictable flight and absorb less water.

Sizing UP the Competition

So just how does the regulation-size soccer ball compare to some oversized giants? Here's how they stack up.

america's record hailstone

At a weight of 1 2/3 pounds, the largest hailstone ever measured in the United States fell at Coffeyville, Kansas, on September 3, 1970. It had an 18-inch circumference (about 6 inches across). That would have been some Sno-cone if only someone had been nearby with raspberry syrup. The good news is that the bigger the hail, the fewer hailstones fall in the same area.

a cannon ball

During the Civil War, cannon balls ranged from grape-sized, iron nuggets about 1 inch in diameter that weighed about 1 pound to balls 15 inches in diameter that weighed 318 pounds.

1970

At the 1970 World Cup in Mexico, Adidas makes the first official FIFA ball, adopting the "Buckyball" pattern, named after architect Buckminster Fuller, who pioneered this structure of 12 pentagons and 20 hexagons that fit together into a nearly perfect sphere. The design made it visible for television viewers.

1986

This ball, called the Azteca, is the first polyurethane-coated ball used at a World Cup. The ball is very water resistant. Unlike the earlier Aztec balls, it does not have a losing player's head wrapped inside.

When fans in other countries say "football," they mean "soccer." In America, when we say "football" we mean "football," when we say "soccer" we mean "soccer," and when we say "cricket," we mean an insect that makes a lot of noise at night.

Football and soccer are variations of a game that has had lots of variation itself. Until 1906, even the American game of football was played with a less-pointed ball—the one still used today in rugby.

So why an oblong ball? The truth is, footballs just wouldn't stay round. Once inflated, they were rarely perfectly round, and they tended to change shape during the pounding they endured in a typical game. When timeouts were called, players grabbed a key from the sidelines, unlocked the ball's nozzle (which was tucked inside the ball), and used nothing but lungpower to "pump up" the ball. Of course, forcing air into a taut leather ball takes tremendous force. Players already winded from playing took turns "pumping" their breaths into the football. But toward the game's end, the last "inflator" was tuckered out and had a hard time trying to increase the pressure. So he sometimes gave up and returned a lopsided ball into the game. Eventually that tapered shape

The oldest football was made of rubber and used by a group of Boston high school boys who had recently founded the Oneida Football Club, the first football club in the United States.

became the official look of the ball.

At that time, American football, like rugby, was primarily a running game, with no helmets, no padding, and lots of players getting bonked pretty hard. It was President Teddy Roosevelt who urged the coaches to make the game safer. And so the ends of the ball were made pointier, tapering the ends of the ball by 1 1/2 inches. You might think that would make the game more dangerous, but it actually provided a better grip on the ball, and this extra control allowed accurate, longer passes—including the "long bomb." The game of football took to the air as well as to the ground—and fullbacks have been happy ever since.

Legendary Washington Redskins quarterback Sammy Baugh drops back to pass against the Chicago Bears in Washington on Sept. 13, 1942. (AP Photo)

As for why we continue to call footballs "pigskins," originally, the rubber bladder inside the cowhide covering was, in fact, the bladder of a pig.

Question A Ball

You spot a ball hawk—and you weren't even birdwatching with your Uncle Gary! What did you see?

a.) someone who "hawks" tickets outside a ball game

b.) a species of raptor that feeds on round eggs

c.) a really skillful ball player

d.) someone who keeps stealing the ball—oh, wait, that's a ball HOG

Answer: A ball hawk, depending on the sport, is a talented ball-handler. In football, it's a player who's great at intercepting balls. In baseball, it could be an outfielder who hardly misses a fly. Or it could be a basketball player who steals balls, grabs rebounds, and dribbles like crazy.

"Quote·a·Ball"

"Sure, luck means a lot in football. Not having a good quarterback is bad luck."

—*Don Shula, former Miami Dolphins football coach with his super-star QB Dan Marino*

Football by the Numbers

5,582
the population of Ada, Ohio (in 2000)

150
the number of people in Ada who work for Wilson Sporting Goods, which has made footballs for the NFL since 1941. While many footballs are made in China, India, Pakistan, and the Dominican Republic, the Ada, Ohio, plant is the only place in America dedicated to making only footballs.

A Real Costume BALL!

Calcio Storico, (which translates as "football in costume") is a 500-year-old variation of football that's played in Florence, Italy, every summer. It's the strangest ball game you'll ever witness. Players dress up in 16th-century Italian costumes, parade through the city, meet spectators and officials, and assemble for a 50-minute game at the town square. Each team of 27 combatants meets for a grueling game held on a giant sand playing field, trying to score points as in a typical football game, rushing the ball through the goals, although several referees are needed to break up the fist fights that break out throughout the match. So it's sort of football plus bare-fisted boxing plus a costume ball with blood-spattered costumes.

Meanwhile, thousands of fans cheer, and smoke bombs of various "team colors" explode in the air. Even wackier, the winning team receives a prize of . . . meat—a pile of steaks equal in weight to one of Italy's prized white calves.

3 to 5	**50**	**24 or 36 or 48**	**100**
the number of days it take to make one football	steps to make one football	the number of footballs the home team must supply for an NFL game. (It's two dozen in a domed stadium, and three dozen in an open-air stadium—but usually fewer than half are used). And then add twelve more balls, officially marked with a "K," for the kicking game.	the cost in dollars of one football ($50 wholesale) 

The Football Plant

As you might guess, footballs don't grow on trees. Here's a quick guide to how a football is constructed.

1. The first of 50 steps (we'll leave out a few) begins with cowhide, a piece of leather that's been tanned and treated to be water-resistant. Four football-shaped panels are cut and trimmed from each hide. One or more logos are stamped in the leather.

2. A lining is sewn to the underside of each panel. This three-ply fabric protects the bladder and supports the ball's shape. Since laces need holes, two panels are hole-punched and then reinforced with another small lining. The valve for inflating the ball is popped in now.

3. A heavy-duty, lockstitch sewing machine binds all four panels together, inside out, leaving a small opening.

4. A strong man then turns the football right-side out. Steaming the leather to soften it and prying with a steel bar, the man slides a bladder through the lace opening. Whew!

5. The ball is closed with heavy linen thread and then "premolded" by inflating the ball with 80 pounds of pressure. That stretches the ball and aligns the seams.

6. A little air is released, and the ball is then double-laced with grid cord—a tough material that can stand up to being rubbed in the mud, crushed between 250-pound dudes, and regularly kicked in the stitches.

7. Finally the ball is fully inflated and the inspections begin! That means carefully evaluating the length, shape, weight, seams, and appearance.

No wonder it can take an entire crew of talented workers almost a week to make a single football. It's an amazing bit of architecture, harnessing that air pressure inside a perfectly balanced, leakproof, leather covering.

1,000,000	**3,000**	**60,000,000**	**0**
the number of footballs made by Wilson in a year (They supply the NFL and many college teams.)	the number of cows needed to produce the leather for one season of footballs for the NFL	pounds of manure those 3,000 cows produce in a year	the number of balls Charlie Brown was able to kick in all his years of comic strip games

THE INSIDE SCOOP

The cloth lining
helps the ball hold its shape.

The bladder
is rubber inflated with air to a pressure that must be 12 1/2 to 13 1/3 pounds. Refs test each ball with a pressure gauge two hours before kickoff time.

Prolate spheroid
is the term for the ball's shape, which means oblong and pointy. (Some college and high school balls have white stripes around the tips to help with visibility.)

The middle circumference is 20 3/4 to 21 1/4 inches.

The tip-to-tip circumference is 28 to 28 1/2 inches.

Laces
eight raised white ones are in the center.

Cowhide leather
panels are natural tan pebble-grained and sewn together.

The ball's weight
is 14 to 15 ounces, just less than one pound.

The length
is 11 to 11 1/2 inches.

BALL of FAME

GOLD POSTS!

Who: Jason Elam of the Denver Broncos
Event: He kicked the longest field goal.
Record: 63 yards in 1999
What's So Great: One of the best kickers in history, Elam is unrivaled when it comes to kicking field goals and scoring extra points.

MEN WITH THE GOLDEN ARMS

Who: NFL quarterbacks: Frank Filchock (1939), George Izo (1963), Karl Sweetan (1966), Sonny Jurgensen (1968), Jim Plunkett (1983), Ron Jaworski (1985), Stan Humphries (1994), Brett Favre (1995), and Trent Green (2002)
Event: They are tied for the longest pass.
Record: 99 yards—that's 1 yard less than the entire length of the field!

PUNT PERSON

Who: Steve O'Neal of the New York Jets
Event: He kicked the longest punt.
Record: 98 yards in 1969
What's So Great: Remember, a punt is not a kick-off with a "teed up" ball and the opposing team safely at the other end of the field. This is catching a snapped ball and kicking it while a bunch of giants are charging!

OOPS!

Who: Warren Moon
Event: He made the most fumbles in a career.
Record: 161 fumbles. In his 16 years of playing for Houston, Minnesota, Seattle, and Kansas City, Warren fumbled the ball more than anyone. But I wouldn't call him Butterfingers if I were you, because . . .
What's So Ironic: Warren also holds the NFL record for the most *recovered* fumbles: He recovered 56 of his own mess-ups!

BALL TALK

bomb: a long pass sent to a receiver running down the field.

live: description of a ball that's in play once it's been snapped or kicked.

loose: description of a ball that's been fumbled or punted.

dead: description of the ball once the play is over.

spiral: a thrown or kicked ball that has a spin, making it travel with more distance and accuracy.

spike: a ball thrown at the ground in the end zone to celebrate a touchdown.

QUESTION A BALL

Say you're going out for a pass—go long!—and you're running hard to catch the ball. (Let's say the quarterback sort of overshot.) Are you more able to catch the ball if . . .

a.) you run at a steady speed and just keep your eye on the ball?

b.) you suddenly run a little faster or slower as the ball comes within reach?

c.) It doesn't matter because it's just a matter of practice. You've either got butterfingers or you're a good receiver.

Answer: Well, receivers, the answer is **b.** When your body leans forward—like a runner just shoving off the starting block—it has more energy and more power. And that is exactly what you need in order to keep your balance and turn quickly to catch that falling ball. Running at a steady pace simply gives you less maneuverability.

What's yellow, fuzzy, and every dog's favorite toy? **LOOK!**

The Tennis Ball!

ACTUAL SIZE!

(Dog slobber optional!)

Some historians say the ancient Egyptians—or was it the Greeks?—no, wait! It was the Romans who played the first game in which a ball was swatted back and forth between players. But most "tennis-torians" say that it was some 12th-century monks of the Basque region of France who created the first tennis-like game.

Their game balls were animal skins stuffed with fleece (that's leather filled with wool), and the game was played against a wall in a courtyard. Competitors smacked the ball with their hands and said, "Ouch!" The ball was pretty hard—and players were often injured if hit by an oncoming ball. After a few centuries of trying different kinds of gloves, players eventually picked up the idea of using a racquet instead.

Later, in the 16th century, Kings Henry VII and Henry VIII of England were fans of the game. They used lighter balls with cork centers that weighed about 3 ounces—a little heavier than present-day balls. Their indoor courts had drooping nets, oddly angled surfaces, and openings

In 1874, Major Walter Wingfield invented the sport of lawn tennis.

on the walls that players could use for bank shots and unpredictable returns.

In the early 1800s, tennis balls were made of wool strips wound around and around and then tied with strings wrapped in all directions to form a core. Finally, a white cloth was sewn over the ball as an outer covering. This old tennis ball looked more like a baseball!

Then, in 1874, Major Walter Wingfield developed modern tennis—the game we play today. He moved the play out onto the grass and used balls made from rubber, created by a process invented by Charles Goodyear (yep, the tire guy again).

Since then, any changes made to the tennis ball have been minor—although dogs probably think the new minty-flavored bouncers are quite an improvement!

"Mmmm, minty fresh!"

WHere Have all THe Tennis Balls gone?

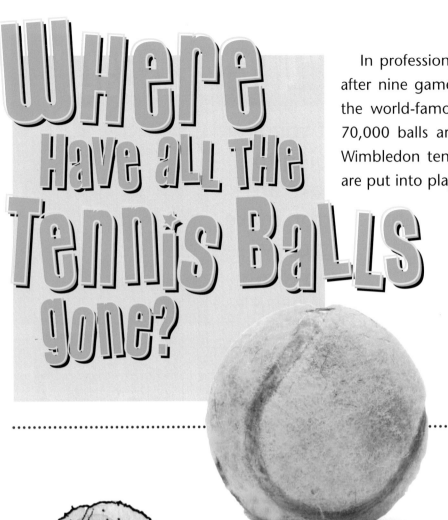

In professional competition, tennis balls are retired after nine games. New balls for every match! During the world-famous tennis matches at the U.S. Open, 70,000 balls are used. In England, at the legendary Wimbledon tennis championship, 31,200 tennis balls are put into play for the main events.

Tennis-ball manufacturers say that after two weeks of normal whacking, smacking, bouncing, and "sproing"ing (even by us amateurs), most tennis balls are "unplayable." That's because the ball's surface gets flattened and its bounce deadens.

Then what? See page 41 for some things to do with old tennis balls.

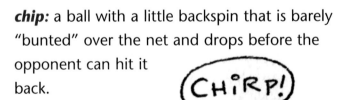

BALL TALK

moon ball: a high lob that leaves your racket on a course to the moon, which is often used to slow the pace of a game. It's also one of those high flyers that goes rocketing out of bounds.

daisy cutter: an oncoming ball with a very low bounce that barely skims the ground, making it pretty hard to return. (It's so low, it could cut down a row of daisies—this is, if you were playing tennis in your dad's flower bed.)

chip: a ball with a little backspin that is barely "bunted" over the net and drops before the opponent can hit it back.

chop: a ball hit with a downward chop, giving it a backwards spin that's a challenge to return.

chirp: the sound of a bird distracting you as you're reaching to hit the ball.

CHiRP!

THE INSIDE SCOOP

Wool or felt covering
is either stain-resistant for grass courts or heavy-duty to resist the extra wear of rougher, outdoor courts.

The air inside
some new balls is nitrogen, which leaks more slowly. Other new balls are called "pressureless"; the rubber core provides all the bounce.

Squishability
is an important factor. Squeezed with 18 pounds of pressure, balls are allowed to dent only about 1/4 of an inch or bulge about 1/3 of an inch.

Elastic sealant
closes each seam of the covering.

Two pieces of rubber core
are cemented together to create a shell.

The ball's weight
must be between 2 and 2 1/16 ounces.

The diameter
is between 2 1/2 and 2 5/8 inches in diameter.

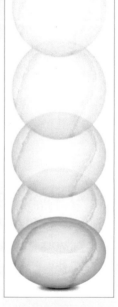

Bounce-ability
is also important. A tennis ball dropped from a height of 100 inches onto a 4-inch thick slab of concrete must bounce between 53 and 58 inches. That's about halfway back—a 50% rebound rate.

The Handball!

ACTUAL SIZE!

(Not a football or a knuckleball
or an eyeball . . .)

Handball (which is played with gloves, so you never actually "touch" the ball), and its cousins—squash, paddleball, and racquetball (all played with racquets)—have so many relatives in the "tennis" family of games that everyone has to wear name badges at the family reunion!

People simply enjoy whacking balls! It doesn't matter if the game is played with teams, in pairs, or one-on-one. It doesn't matter if it's played indoors or outdoors or on a court with four walls or just one front wall. And the star of all these games is a small, speedy ball that's a ricocheting demon.

Smacked against roofs, doors, and courtyards, the early handballs were leather pouches stuffed with dirt, sawdust, or even dog hair. As for the first racquets, they were often nothing more than sticks, branches, shepherd crooks or—who knows?—the garden trowel or the kitchen spatula. It wasn't until the 15th century that the Dutch created the first real racquets.

Which leads to a good question: Is it "rackets" or "racquets"? It's your choice, really. But just to make things more confusing, both of these English words come from the French, who borrowed them from the Italian, who took them from an Arabic word that means "palm of the hand." Now *that's* wacky!

Wearing protective eyewear and a sweat-soaked head band, a player tries to keep his eye on that tiny ball while actually hitting it with his hand.

Nowadays many official and unofficial forms of this ball-slamming sport are played by using bare hands, gloved hands, long or short racquets, and long or short courts (including streets, stoops, and parking lots). Many of the different leagues and games have their own regulation ball, each of which is designed to suit the game. But this ball, the standard handball of the United States Handball Association, should give you a basic idea of how these little speedballs are put together.

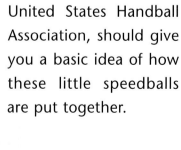

QUESTION A BALL

Each time a ball collides with something—a wall, the floor, your racket or glove—it indents, springs back, and takes off with whatever energy it still has left. Which of these other things also happens to the ball as the game wears on? The ball gets...

   a.) warm, warmer—wow, that's actually hot!

   b.) softer, smooshier, and more flexible.

   c.) more bounce to the ounce.

   d.) a really awful headache.

Answer: Other than the fact that the ball doesn't know if it has a headache, **all** of the other answers are correct. In every collision, a ball deforms and re-forms. Some of the ball's molecules crowd together and some spread apart to change the ball's shape, and they create heat by working that hard. This work uses up energy that the ball has gained from being hit. If the ball didn't heat up, the energy would still be part of its rebounding force. Not to worry, though, because the ball gets more flexible as it heats up, and that adds some extra bouncing power.

THE INSIDE SCOOP

The exterior
is rubber or another synthetic material of any color. Its thickness is less than 1/3 of an inch.

Air
that is not pressurized is inside. Basically a handball is hollow, rather than filled with air like a basketball.

The diameter
is 1 7/8 inches, but a 1/32 inch variation is permitted.

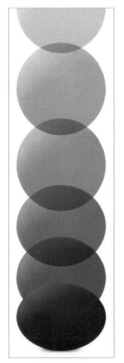

The weight
is between 2.04 and 2.18 ounces (58 to 62 grams) with a .07 ounce (2 gram) variation permitted.

Bounce-ability
is critical because players count on the ball's ricocheting ability. When dropped on a hardwood floor from a height of 70 inches, the ball must rebound between 48 and 52 inches at 68°F. This gives the ball a 70% bounce factor.

How to Cook Up a Handball

So what's the recipe for a handball? Not that you can make one in your own kitchen, but the process really is more like making a hollow chocolate Easter bunny than sewing up a football.

1.) Start with raw rubber. You can find that on your next trip to Malaysia. You'll want to soften the rubber-tree sap by "mastication" (which is what your jaws do to the food you eat), using a machine that chews on the rubber. Next, add in a few powders, fillers, polymers, more fillers, colors, and other closely guarded secret ingredients to create a strong, colorful, resilient compound.

2.) Warm this compound and pack it into an extruder. (Think of a goliath pasta machine.) Using a rotating blade, snip the ropes of the extruded putty into pellets.

3.) Place each pellet on a hydraulic press and squeeze it at a pressure of 1,100 pounds per square inch for 12 minutes, while cooking it at about 150°F. You now have a half shell: one side of a handball. The press makes two kinds of shells: the "dots," which have a small dimple at the bottom to which a dot of paint will adhere, and the "plains," which don't.

4.) Trim away any excess putty from the edges and then grind the edges to roughen them up so the glue will stick. Apply one coat of adhesive, wait thirty minutes, and then repeat this process two more times. Go ahead and dab on the dot of paint as well.

5.) Now stick the two halves together (a process called "flapping"), and then pop the ball into another press for a second molding and curing: 1000 pounds per square inch for 15 minutes. This hardens the seam and strengthens the ball's shape.

6.) Now buff the ball to smooth the seam and create an even surface. Wash it, dry it, and let one of the inspectors give it a few tests. Finally, stamp the ball with a logo. It's ready to smack around.

A Ball for Every Player

Dunlap makes 90% of the squash balls in the world. They've developed four balls with special properties—one for each kind of player.

1. The Single Yellow Dot: This standard-size ball is black with a single yellow dot and has 10% more hang time, which means it doesn't bounce back quite as fast. It "hangs" in the air a little longer. For competitors.

2. The Double Yellow Dot: The official ball of many associations, this is the standard-size black ball with a double yellow dot. For professionals.

> *Other manufacturers create balls of different colors and specifications for each variation of this sport in order that players of all levels can compete to the best advantage.*

3. The Practice Ball: This ball is 6% larger, with 20% longer "hang time." It's a ball with "instant bounce"; it doesn't need to be warmed up during practice in order to have the right bounce. For serious players who are in competitions.

4. The Basic Blue: This blue ball is 12% larger, with 40% greater "hang time," which makes it easier to hit. With "instant bounce," the ball is designed for kids and beginners.

BALL TALK

around-the-wall shot: a ball that ricochets from one side wall of the court to the front wall and then to the other side wall.

back-into-back-wall shot: a ball that's hit hard into the rear wall so that it flies all the way to the front wall.

down-the-line shot: a returning ball that's very close to a side wall, which, when struck back into the front wall, bounces right back along the same side wall.

pinch shot: a ball shot low into a front corner that hits the side wall and then the front wall.

splat: a ball slammed from near one side of the court to the other side wall.

wallpaper shot: a shot that travels close to a side wall without touching it.

Z ball: a ball whose flight is a zigzagging "Z." It hits the front wall, one sidewall, the other side wall, and then sails toward the back wall.

QUESTION A BALL

PLAYING GAMES IN SPACE

What sign did John Glenn post on the instrument panel of Freedom 7, the first human-piloted craft the United States launched into space?

a.) "I ♥ squash."

b.) "No handball playing here."

c.) "Racquetball rules!"

d.) "If you're happy and you know it, clap your hands."

e.) "Earth's just one little malted milk ball rolling around the Milky Way."

Answer: **b**. On May 5, 1961, Alan Shepard piloted the seventh Mercury capsule for 15 minutes and 28 seconds, reaching 116.5 miles into space at a speed of 5,134 miles per hour. His fellow astronaut, John Glenn, posted the sign because handball had been a part of their physical conditioning during training.

Astronaut John H. Glenn Jr. in his silver Mercury spacesuit during pre-flight training activities at Cape Canaveral on February 20, 1962.

What has dimples but no smile, is sometimes lost at sea, and often has sand kicked in its face?

47

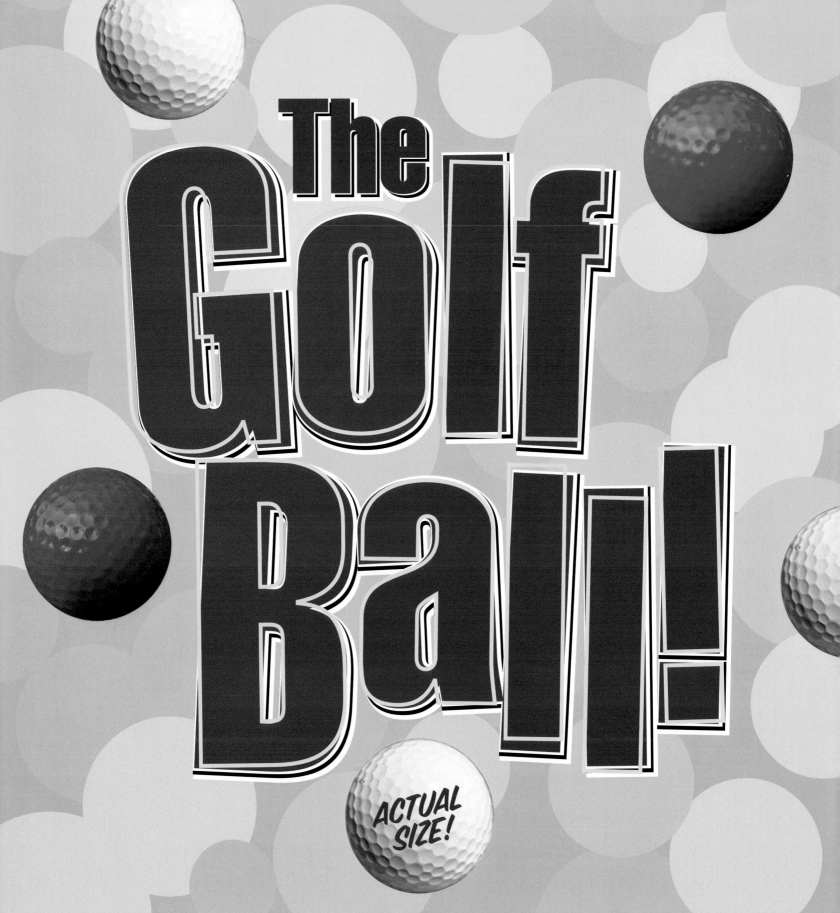

The Golf Ball!

ACTUAL SIZE!

(The ball that loves to get teed off!)

Human beings everywhere seem to have a need to hit little balls with little sticks into little holes. During the time of Caesar, Romans used club-shaped branches to whack balls stuffed with feathers in a game called *paganica*. Artifacts suggest that people in Japan, France, Italy, and England each created a similar game of ball and clubs at about the same time. In Holland, in about the 13th century, skaters on ice played "kolf." In Scotland, stories are told of a shepherd who invented the game using his crook to knock pebbles into a rabbit hole while watching his flock. (And you thought *you* were bored!)

Eventually golf became the game of kings—because few other folks could afford the game! A single golf ball could cost between 150 and 400 of today's dollars. Bringing the necessary six balls to a game could cost more than $2,000, which the king's subjects were unlikely to have most weekends. (These days, Americans spend more than $630 million a year on golf balls, each of which typically costs between 50 cents and 5 dollars.) Ironically, in 1457 King James banned the game because his archers were hitting balls instead of practicing their military exercises.

British golfers 'Old' Tom Morris and Charlie Hunter at a match at Prestwick, Ayrshire Scotland, site of the first professional golf tournament, held in 1860. Eight golfers entered. 'Old' Tom and his son 'Young' Tom became the only father and son to hold successive open titles in 1867 and 1868.

Over the years, some manufacturing advances have created balls that can spin 8,000 times in a minute, fly 300 yards, and travel at speeds of 170 miles per hour—or even roll through the chomping jaws of a concrete crocodile or the whirring blades of a windmill! There are even golf balls that light up when hit and flash for five minutes so you can find them in the dark.

The Change-a-Ball Golf Ball

Golf balls haven't always been the cute little dimpled darlings we whack, whiff, and putt on grass that's groomed closer than a man's beard, lose in a forest, sink in a pond, and toss in washing machines today. (No kidding, used golf balls often churn around in the wash cycle to create a softened, faded fabric. You might even own a pair of "golf ball-washed" jeans.) Yes, the golf ball has had a few makeovers in its long history.

stone ball

Most golf historians credit the invention of golf to an unknown Scottish shepherd who used his staff to putt a round rock into a hole. The earliest golfers probably hit balls made of stone. The earliest golf spectators—this is well before the age of binoculars—wisely watched from far, far away. During the 1500s, chicken and goose feathers were boiled and then stuffed inside 2 or 4 leather strips sewn with waxed thread, and then the ball was dried and painted white. It probably made sense: If feathers could help a bird fly, what could they do for a golf ball? According to the British Golf Museum, these golf balls, called featheries, could "fly" about 160 yards.

feathery ball

In those days, the clubs were long and flat, so basically they were all wooden "putters." Early golf games were played on working farmlands, so balls sometimes landed in some tough places, like deep wagon ruts or tracks. Rules didn't allow the golfer to "improve his lie," by moving the ball, so a new kind of club had to be invented to hit the ball from those deep spots. Golf's first iron was a short-faced club used to get the ball out of the rut or track. Thus, the names "rut iron" and "track iron."

Because it took three or four hours to make a single ball, losing or damaging those balls before you finished a game was a real problem. So a different kind of ball was needed.

guttie ball

In 1848, the ball made of sap appeared. The gutta-percha (also know as the "guttie") ball was formed from the dried black sap of the Malaysian sapodilla tree and painted white. These molded balls could be driven a bit farther, so courses were made longer. In addition, clubs were made shorter, and broader irons became popular. Many of these balls could be made quickly. After golfers realized that a scuffed ball made the ball fly farther, balls were marked or molded with patterns or dents. Iron molds pressed a variety of patterns into the balls, each pattern an attempt to improve the distance and way in which the ball traveled. One of the most popular balls was covered with bumps like a berry. It was called the "bramble ball."

rubber ball

By 1898, rubber bounced onto the fairway. The golf ball had rubber threads wound around a rubber core, wrapped in a gutta-percha cover, and coated with enamel paint. By

Odd Balls

1. EcoBall

Made of compressed rawhide and other organic materials, this eco-friendly golf ball travels about 75% as far as a regular golf ball off the tee (which also comes in a biodegradable material). But now golfers can thwack buckets of balls into the ocean and not pollute the waters. The ball decomposes in four days, offering up organic tidbits for marine life. Even the Navy offers EcoBall golfing aboard ship to help sailors unwind.

switching to this new ball, a golfer usually gained about 15 yards—the ball traveling as much as 180 to 250 yards on a drive. These better balls not only traveled farther, but once the dimples were added, they could fly straighter, offering the player more control. Clubs were made of harder woods, or larger irons with grooved faces, all of which improved the ball's spin and distance. The most popular woods were hickory (for the club's shaft) and persimmon, apple, or pear (for the club's head).

The golf tee was first patented by Dr. George Grant in 1899.

By the early 1900s, the first golf tees were created, so golfers didn't have to drive the ball off wet mounds of sand. Standards for the golf balls themselves were first set by the British in 1930, and then by the U.S. in 1932. Players in the U.S. used slightly larger balls, but the British held onto their smaller standard because of the winds in their region. Finally, in 1990, the Brits accepted the U.S. standard ball as theirs, too.

1960s composite ball

More improvements came in the 1960s when a two-piece ball composed of a solid core inside a tough, synthetic cover called Surlyn, which was based on *balata*, a rubber-like gum from a tropical tree. This ball traveled an even greater distance, although golfers lost a little control and spin.

After this innovation, companies experimented with all kinds of centers, including a rubber sac filled with water, lead, glue, glycerin, and even tapioca. Yes, the pudding.

In the future, new creations of golf balls will include those with a titanium shell with a hollow center. The weight is moved from the center of the ball to the outside by using nanostructures (objects that are only a few billionths of a meter). This shift of weight cuts down on the sidespin (which is what sends balls off course), but doesn't cause the ball to lose much backspin. It's like when a spinning skater slows down by extending his or her arms. Driving distances may not only keep getting longer, but may become straighter and straighter, too.

2. SNOWBALL

The English writer Rudyard Kipling invented snow golf while living in Vermont. He painted his golf balls red so he could find them. (While we're speaking of snowballs, it might be "cool" to know that the largest snowball fight on record took place in Switzerland in 2003, when 2,473 people hammered each other with snowballs for ten minutes. If you have 2,474 friends, you could break their record!)

QUESTiON A BALL

Four! I Mean, Fore!

In eighteen holes of golf, how much total time do the ball and the various clubs spend touching? In other words, what is the total "whack time" for a complete game of golf?

a.) 40 seconds

b.) 4 seconds

c.) The same time as the number of licks it takes to get to the center of a Tootsie Pop

d.) 1/2 second or less

Answer: For all the hours a golfer spends on the course—walking, practicing swings, lining up shots, chasing balls, shouting *fore!* and waiting for the ball to land—the total time that the clubs are touching the ball on eighteen holes is less than half a second. So the right answer is **d.**

If You Were a Golf Ball . . .

"My sister has dimples and I don't. Does that mean she could fly farther than I if we were golf balls?"

All right, if she were completely round and if dimples covered her entire body instead of just dotting each side of her smile, the answer is *yes*. She, like a dimpled golf ball that travels through the air, has to push against the air while the air pushes back. That's known as *air friction*. (Golfing in water would result in even more friction, which is only one reason underwater golf hasn't become popular.) This air friction causes resistance, which slows every kind of flying ball, dimpled or not.

But the real drag—literally!—comes from how the air separates *behind* your dimpled sister-ball. This pressure, known as drag, acts like a sucking vacuum cleaner behind the ball. But if a ball has dimples or scratches, the flow behind the ball is turbulent—little bits of air cling to the ball like a little whirlwind—forcing the ball farther.

And there's another factor to consider. If you were a smooth golf ball, and you were *spinning*, then you might out-distance your dimpled sister if she weren't spinning. Most golf balls spin a lot—some as much as 133 times per second—which lifts them into the air.

3. MOONBALL Not yet a real PGA sport (in fact, only one ball has yet been shot up there), moon golf sounds like a great game. With less gravity, a ball can travel huge distances with just a little *fwap*! Astronaut Alan Shepard, while wearing a bulky spacesuit, hit a ball 200 yards with a 6-iron. But the longest *earthly* flight of a golf ball launched on a golf course is 458 yards, sent into orbit by America's Jack Hamm while playing in Colorado. FORE! (Or even FIVE!)

THE INSIDE SCOOP

The cover
is made of hard rubber or synthetic material and is nearly always dimpled.

The dimples
increase the ball's speed. Most golf balls have between 300 and 450 dimples. Patterns vary. Golfers often have favorite balls that are best-suited to their style of play. The typical dimple is 7/1000 of an inch deep.

The ball's weight
must be 1.62 ounces.

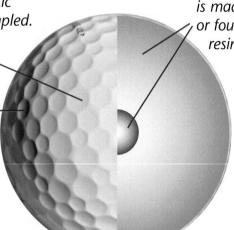

The molded core
is made of rubber or even two, three, or four layers of wound rubber threads, resins, or and other materials.

The flight factor
means no ball can travel more than 280 yards when hit by Iron Byron— the United States Golf Association's mechanical golfer! A ball also can't travel more than 250 feet per second as it leaves the tee. Byron's balls spin 42 times per second.

The diameter
must be 1.68 inches across.
(The hole on the green is 4.25 inches wide.)

"quote·a·ball"

Perhaps more than in any other ball sport, golfers seem to have something profound to say about this frustrating game.

"I know I'm getting better at golf because I'm hitting fewer spectators." —*former President Gerald Ford*

"If you think it's hard to meet new people, try picking up the wrong golf ball." —*actor Jack Lemmon*

◄ "Golf is the only sport where the ball doesn't move until you hit it." —*baseball great Ted Williams*

---

4. POND BALL
Retrieving golf balls from waterholes, ponds, and streams is a real business. These "pond balls" can be spiffed up, polished, and resold. Sound like panning for gold? Reselling used golf balls is a $200-million-a-year business.

5. BUCKETS OF FUN
According to the National Golf Association, a driving range's extra-large golf-ball bucket contains about 150 balls, a large bucket holds 90 balls, a medium bucket contains 63 balls, and a small bucket provides a mere 35 balls. And a quarter-cup of golf balls would be one ball. Slice away!

BALL of FAME

Golfing Tiger, Hidden Camera

Who: Tiger Woods
Event: Swing speed
What's So Great: A hot-shot ball, that's what! On average, a good golfer can swing a club at the speed of 100 miles per hour. (Special photographic techniques can assess a player's swing speed, even though the club isn't traveling for an entire mile.) Tiger can swing at 125 miles per hour and averages about 292 yards off the tee. That "launch" velocity can reach 160 miles per hour—20 miles per hour faster than a great tennis serve.

Power Driver

Who: Paul Slater
Event: Length of drive off a tee
Where: London City Airport's tarmac (not what you'd call a real golf course)
What's So Great: Paul drove a golf ball 720 yards, two or three times the length of most professional golfers' best drives off the tee. That's more than seven football fields long!

It Can Be Done

Who: Don Athey of Bridgeport, CT
What: Stacked 9 golf balls, one on top of the other without using glue or anything!
What's So Great: He practiced 20 times a week for 18 years. How many can you stack?

Pucker Up

Who: The Dimplit Golf Ball
Record: Having 1,070 dimples on one ball: 656 pinhead-sized dimples and 414 larger dimples.

What's So Great: The most dimples on any of the 765 USGA-approved balls—more than *twice* the number of a typical ball. And by the way: Every ball type but one currently manufactured has an even number of dimples. The "odd ball" has 333.

BALL TALK

ace: a hole in one.

airball: when you swing at the ball and the ball is in the same place after your swing. Sorry, you missed.

hairball: kitty's little bit of upchuck—not all that useful on a golf course, of course.

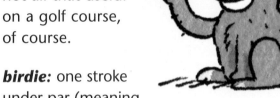

birdie: one stroke under par (meaning, the ball sinks into the hole in one less stroke than the hole's predicted difficulty); also, one of kitty's favorite targets.

bird's nest: a ball that's lying in a place where it is not easy to play, something like a clump of deep grass or weeds, like an egg in a nest.

banana ball: a ball that curves like a banana, sailing off-course because the club "sliced" the ball rather than hit it squarely.

bowker: a ball that bonks a spectator or a tree and bounces back into play. Not a planned shot, exactly, but President Ford was good at these.

dead ball: a ball that's so close to the hole that the player's next putt can't possibly miss.

grasscutter: either a solid shot flying low and long across the course (or one of the guys who keeps the greens nicely mown).

Shake, rattle, and run!

A rattlesnake and a golfer met on a golf course—hey, it's no joke! There are rules about things like this. So what happens if your ball lands near a rattlesnake? The official rules state: *". . . the Player must not play the Ball from this Position. He may drop a second Ball in reasonable distance to the Reptile, but not closer to the Pin. The player gets no penalty stroke . . . ."*

It's good to know that there's no penalty for moving the ball in order not to get bitten by a rattler. And if your ball lands near poison ivy, cactus, a "biting shrub or burning nettle," you are also allowed to move the ball—but you have to take a penalty stroke. Now *that* could rattle a golfer, for sure.

What goes bump, set, spike; bump, set, kill; bump, set, dump?

LOOK!

The Volleyball!

Baby, can you dig it?
Or dink it?

ACTUAL SIZE!

A true, all-American invention, volleyball began in Holyoke, Massachusetts, at a YMCA in 1895, when William G. Morgan devised a team sport that involved hitting a basketball back and forth over a tennis net set slightly taller than the average Joe, 6' 6" high. He was shooting for a game that was less strenuous than basketball, one that businessmen and "older" YMCA members could enjoy. (Which also explains why they hoisted up a tennis net and tossed a basketball onto the court at first—the actual volleyball itself came five years later, in 1900.)

Originally the game was called *mintonette*, a French word meaning "little mintons." (Mintons are—well, Mr. Morgan wasn't sure, but he had heard of the name "badminton" and dreamed up a fancier version of that!) A year later, the name changed to volleyball, and everyone was quite relieved.

The first rules of the game described the ball as "a rubber bladder covered with leather or canvas, not less than 25 inches nor more than 27 inches in circumference, weight between 9 and 12 ounces." It's also interesting that the original game had nine "innings" like baseball and had "dribbling." But unlike basketball, *this* dribbling was a legal maneuver where a player bounced the ball up and down on his hands or arms while moving.

In the early 1920s, beach volleyball—the same game with six players in brightly colored bathing trunks on a sandy court—started up in Santa Monica, California. A little sand, a little sun, and a <u>LOT</u> of sunburn!

Today, more than 800 million people play some form of volleyball around the world at least once a week, making it the second-most-popular sport after soccer. There's even a variation called mini-volleyball for kids 6 to 12 that's played on a smaller court with a lower, 6-foot-high net and a smaller ball. Invented in Canada, mini-volleyball is especially popular in Europe and Australia.

Meanwhile, the actual volleyball ball itself hasn't changed drastically in its eleven decades. Like its ancestor, the basketball, the volleyball has continued to evolve as its basic materials improve. Volleyball designers are always searching for improvements. They want to find better ways to treat, replace, or add strength to the ball's leather; to create more resilient linings; and to improve the bladder's ability to hold air. Oh, and they also want to create cool designs and logos on the balls.

THE INSIDE SCOOP

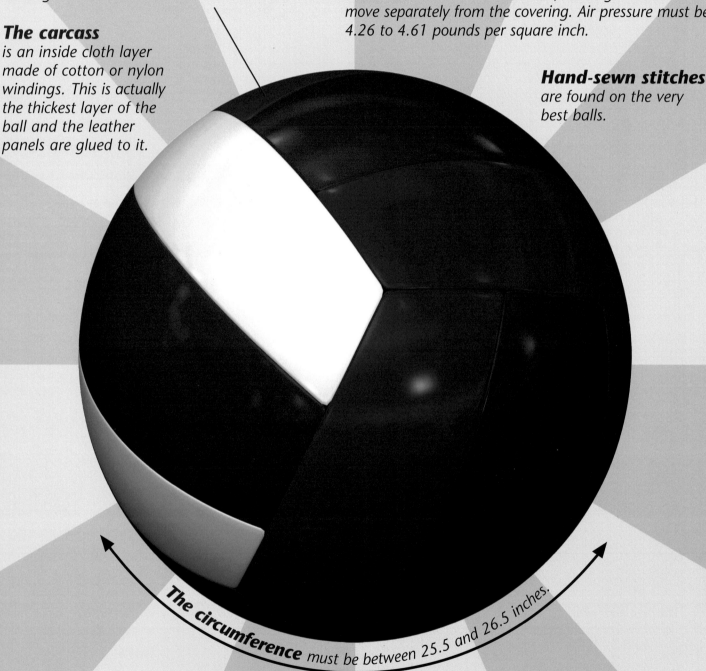

The spherical covering
is made of flexible leather or synthetic leather panels, usually 18 of them. The color can be one solid light color or a combination of colors.

The carcass
is an inside cloth layer made of cotton or nylon windings. This is actually the thickest layer of the ball and the leather panels are glued to it.

The bladder
is rubber or a similar material. This is the same stuff a bike's inner tube is made of and is filled with air. The best balls have a bladder that "floats," letting the bladder move separately from the covering. Air pressure must be 4.26 to 4.61 pounds per square inch.

Hand-sewn stitches
are found on the very best balls.

The circumference must be between 25.5 and 26.5 inches.

The ball's weight
must be between 9 and 10 ounces. (Leagues for younger players often use smaller, lighter balls.) Balls need to be perfectly balanced in order to fly, spin, and retain air pressure.

BALL TALK

dink: a soft, one-handed hit using the fingertips to tap the ball over the net.

duck: what a spectator is supposed to do with a really wild serve.

floater: a served ball that has no spin and floats over the net. It's the unpredictable "knuckleball" of volleyball.

free ball: a ball returned to your opponent without an intent to kill—just an easy pass rather than a spike.

line shot: a spiked ball that lands right on the boundary line of the other team's court—and "on the line" means "good" in volleyball.

pancake: if the back of your hand were a spatula and the volleyball were a pancake, and if you were sliding into home plate at the same time, you'd be executing a pancake—a dive with one hand extended to save the ball from touching the court.

rainbow: a ball that arches like a rainbow, gliding over the front-row blockers toward the back line.

six-packed: when the ball delivers a wicked whack right in your face—*yowch!* (And there is also the chester—a ball smacked squarely in your chest. *Ooooph!*)

spike: a ball slammed down over the net onto the opponent's side—a big attempt to score.

stuff: a spike an opponent blocks, sending it right back to the other team's floor.

"Quote·a·Ball"

"…the serve is the only technique that is totally under your control."

—*Karch Kiraly, volleyball superstar*

BALL of FAME

Star Volleyball

Who: Wilson, the volleyball star of the movie *Cast Away*, was stranded on a desert island with Tom Hanks's character. The two become best buddies. (As if they really had a choice.)

Record: The ball sold at auction for $18,400.

When: 2001

Who's So Great: Mr. Hanks was not auctioned, although he did receive a cool $20 million dollars as part of his earnings for that movie, and he re-

mains one of the most sought-after actors in Hollywood. Meanwhile Wilson's career is clearly washed up. Three actual Wilson volleyballs were used when filming the movie.

Player of the Centuries

Who: Karsh Kiraly

Born: November 3, 1960

Record: With 147 career victories as of 2005, he's the winningest volleyball player in history.

What's So Great: Quite simply, *he* is! A three-time Olympic gold medalist (two for indoor volleyball and one for beach volleyball), Karsh has earned such titles as Most Valuable Player, Greatest Volleyball Player of the Century, and Best Male Volleyball Player in the World (twice). Oh, and he's also won more money than anyone in the sport: more than $3 million.

Towers of Power

Who: The giants of volleyball.

Record: The tallest volleyball players, both dinkers and slammers.

What's So Great: Since the net in volleyball is so high (for women it stands 7' 4 1/8" from the ground, and for men, it stands 7' 11 5/8" high), tall players have the true advantage. Some of the game's towering figures are Ryan Gandy, the tallest living volleyball player at 7' tall; NBA great, Wilt Chamberlain, the tallest volleyball player ever, who stood 7' 1";

Flo Hyman

Flo Hyman, gold-medalist on the 1984 US Women's Olympic Volleyball Team, who stood 6' 5"; Jennifer Harvey, also 6' 5", who played for Stanford; and, at nearly 6' 10", a young Alana Renaud of St.

Petersburg, Florida, who is just beginning her volleyball career. (Just for comparison, wrestling legend Hulk Hogan and the actor who played Darth Vader, Dave Prowse, are both 6' 7".)

To Every Ball, There is a Season . . .

Let's say you're playing indoor volleyball during the winter, and you serve the ball—perfectly! It sails over the net to the back of your opponent's side of the court. Now, let's pretend you make that exact serve with the same force and the same ball, but this time, you're playing on the beach on a windless summer day. Which ball would travel farther?

a.) *It makes no difference. Volleyballs don't care about weather.*

b.) *The summer ball would travel farther. (Plus, it wouldn't complain about the humidity.)*

c.) *The winter ball would travel farther. (Plus, it wouldn't complain about the cold.)*

Answer: On a hot, humid day, the air is less dense, even though humidity makes it feel thicker to you. And this thinner air decreases the dragging and lifting forces that pull on the ball as it flies. So the volleyball would be able to soar about 5% farther. (Meaning if you hit the "winter" ball 100 feet, the "summer" ball would go 105 feet.) Answer **b** is correct.

On the other hand, humidity can make the ball itself heavier, because the leather absorbs moisture from the air. A "wetter" ball is heavier and doesn't travel as far. So if it were a hot, dry day, the ball would sail farther. But on a hot, humid day . . . maybe not quite as far. Humidity does change a ball's flight. And this applies to just about any ball you whack, throw, kick, or accidentally leave at your friend's house and have to go back and get because it was your older brother's ball that you weren't supposed to be using in the first place.

What can you chop, smash, and push, even if you're not a King-Kong-size bully?

A Table Tennis Ball!

ACTUAL SIZE!

Ping-Pong, anyone?

Talk about a sport that's come a long way! British officers in India and South Africa played the first games of table tennis, the official name of the game we usually call Ping-Pong. These fellows carved balls from bottle corks, improvised paddles from cigar-box lids, and set books across the center of a table for their "net." Eventually players opted for more standard equipment and pretty much gave up smoking cigars.

In the 1880s a British engineer named James Gibbs brought the game—then called *Gossima*—to the United States, along with a few celluloid balls. The game had other names, too: *Flim Flam, Whiff-Whaff,* and *Whip-Whap.* Soon enough, the name "Ping-Pong" came along, hoping to be the only sport to be named after the sound it makes, in this case the sound of the ball bopping the table and the paddle.

When the toy manufacturer Parker Brothers registered the name "Ping-Pong" as a trademark, members of the new American Ping-Pong Association were required to use Parker Brothers' equipment. Soon alternative organizations formed (so they could use other manufacturers' equipment), eventually merging in 1935 to create the U.S. Table Tennis Association (now called U.S.A.

Table tennis in the early 1900s was played right on the dining room table.

Table Tennis). Ping-Pong practically became standard equipment in every American basement in the 1960s. Table tennis finally became an official Olympic sport in 1988.

Table tennis balls are among the few things still made of celluloid, a durable compound invented in 1858 as a substitute for ivory in making billiard balls. (Although celluloid was easy to mold, polish, color, and manufacture, the billiard balls had a nasty tendency to crack, split, and catch fire when the balls clacked together. Talk about an explosive pool match!) Celluloid was also used for many years to create motion picture film, jewelry, and other molded items.

SPIN TO WIN!

During a match, most players use three different spins on their balls, as well as hitting back a few no-spin balls. Typical spin shots can make the ball rotate 170 times in a single second. These three spins are:

1. topspin: a forward-spinning ball created by applying an upward stroke on the back of the ball. Using topspin is a good attacking move because it can make the ball . . .

- *travel downward with real force;*
- *bounce up quickly, making your opponent miscalculate the ball's position;*
- *tricky for your opponent to return—it's easy to hit the ball too high or off the table's edge.*

2. backspin: a backward spin caused by applying a downward stroke to the back of the ball. It sends the ball forward, but with a backspin (also called a chop or underspin). A good defensive move, backspin can make the ball . . .

- *go low and long (the backspin makes the ball curve up, while gravity makes it curve down);*
- *slow or pause after its bounce;*
- *difficult to return without hitting it into net.*

3. sidespin: a ball that rotates sideways, like a globe, caused by hitting the back of the ball with a sideways chop. An especially good addition to a serve, sidespin can make the ball . . .

- *veer to the left or right, which can be hard for your opponent to predict;*
- *bounce sideways off the table;*
- *hard to return unless your opponent takes the spin into account—watch out for wayward balls!*

Star POWer

Most table tennis balls have stars—and not because they've been bopped one too many times. The stars tell you each ball's grade. Official tournament balls have three stars. They're the best quality, best balanced, and truest fliers. Two-star balls are the next best; they're used in practice games or for recreational players. The one-star balls are cheaper and perform less consistently. Some balls get no stars at all, because they're not made to professional standards.

Small Change = Better Games

In 2000, the size of a table tennis ball was officially increased two millimeters. The International Table Tennis Foundation figured that the jump from 38 to 40 millimeters would reduce the ball's speed by up 8% and slow its spin as much as 13%. Why make such a small change? The increasing skill of the players and the improvements in the paddle's surface were creating games with such speed that rallies were short, the balls were hard to see (especially on television), and spectators were getting dizzy!

The Ball's Best Buddy, the Paddle

Players choose paddles, made mostly of wood, to deliver the kinds of shots they like to make. Some want more speed, some more smashing or spinning ability, and some just want a paddle for all-around play. Paddle size doesn't matter, although teensy paddles or humongous paddles pose obvious problems.

Official paddles are black on one side and cherry-red on the other, which helps players identify what kind of hit may be coming their way. One side is covered with pimpled rubber—little bumps that help grab the ball. Some have a cushioning sponge layer under the rubber. Some have surfaces with the bumps turned in, creating a smooth surface. Many players also apply slow-drying tacky glue to that surface, helping the ball stick.

In a typical stroke, the ball travels less than .667 inch across the racket in less than .001 second.

Scrub-a-Dub-Dub

Don't forget to wash your new Ping-Pong balls! A light powder clings to the outside of brand-new balls. Just wash them quickly in a bath of diluted dish-washing liquid, and then dry them well before playing.

QUESTION A BALL

If you went to the sporting goods store and asked the clerk for a pound of table tennis balls, what would you get?

a.) 16 balls

b.) a strange look from the sales guy—
    balls aren't sold by the pound!

c.) 168

d.) 68

Answer: The correct answer is **c** (although **b** might be true, too). Each ball is barely 1/10th of an ounce, so 16 ounces would be about 168 balls.

THE INSIDE SCOOP

The hollow sphere
is made of celluloid, usually either orange or white.

The official stamp
of the appropriate table tennis association must be on every ball. The logo of its manufacturer is allowed, too.

The seam
joins the two hemispheres and is nearly invisible to the naked eye.

The ball's weight
must be 2.7 grams (that's not even .1 ounces).

Air
fills the center but isn't under pressure.

The diameter
must be 40 millimeters (1.57 inches).

The veer factor
makes sure a ball isn't lopsided or thicker in one spot than another. Each ball is tested three times by rolling it down a short, V-shaped plane. Once the ball leaves the chute, it can't veer off to one side more than 75 millimeters (just over .667 inches).

Bounce-ability
is an important factor. When dropped from a height of 12 inches onto a steel block, the ball must rebound about 75% (between 9.05 and 9.84 inches).

BALL TALK

chop: a defensive shot that carries a tremendous amount of backspin.

dead ball: a ball returned without any spin. It's very difficult to execute and equally hard for your opponent to read and return.

drop shot: a well-hit ball that just barely clears the net, making it very tough to return.

lob: a ball bopped high into the air, often used by a player who needs an extra fraction of time to recover from an opponent's kill shot.

loop: a ball hit with a large, upward motion of the paddle, giving it a lot of topspin. This often makes the returned ball bounce very high—which is perfect to slam right back!

kerplunk: the sound of a Ping-Pong ball splashing in a small goldfish bowl. (Not officially recognized by the International Table Tennis Federation.)

push: a defensive shot used to successfully return backspin shots. In this case the racket is "open" (tilted upward, away from the table) to lift the backspin over the net.

skunk: an informal rule in table tennis that says that a player wins a game at a score of 7-0 or 11-1.

smash: an offensive, high-speed shot used against high balls. Also called a "kill."

The Vanishing Ball

Magicians like to make Ping-Pong balls disappear from their hands or pockets and then reappear from their mouths or from behind your ear. Ping-Pong balls are easy to palm and hide. And they're so light they almost defy gravity without so much as a "hocus-pocus." Try this quick trick: Grab a plastic chopstick or other plastic "wand" and rub it for 15 seconds with something made of wool, such as the sleeve of a sweater. (Rubbing creates a negative charge on the wand.) Now bring your wand near a Ping-Pong ball. The ball will instantly move toward it! You've charmed the ball. (Actually, the ball's positive charge is attracted to the wand's negative charge. So much for magic, huh?)

What's the opposite of fewer even squares? LOOK!

67

More ODD Balls

From Beans to Balls

What ball spends its life behind bars with 74 other inmates, wears a number on its back, but has never committed a crime?

If you said "BINGO," you win! In the U.S., seventy-five Ping-Pong balls tumble around inside a Bingo cage from which the caller pulls one ball at a time. In England and Australia, ninety balls are used. All over the world, dozens of other variations on this popular 500-year-old game can be found. Originally, Bingo balls were numbered chips that the caller pulled from a sack.

The game originated in Italy as a kind of lottery called—of all things—Lotto. In Germany, the game was used to help teach children learn math. When the game came to the U.S., it was renamed "Beano," because players used dried beans to cover the numbers on their playing cards. The modern name came along when a winner excitedly shouted "Bingo!" instead of "Beano!" B-4 long, everyone was playing Bingo.

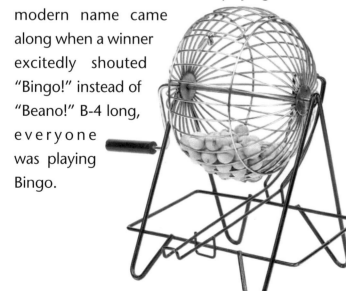

Chinese Health Balls

Worry balls, lotus balls, chiming balls, Qigong balls, miracle balls, therapy balls—these are all names for small (1 3/4 inches), medium (1 15/16 inches), or large (2 3/16 inches) metal balls that you hold in your hand and rotate, using your fingers to move the balls around and around. Some balls are hollow, some solid. Some are metal, some stone. Some have a sounding plate inside that makes them "sing" or chime when rolled or clinked together.

Rolling these little guys in your palm allows you to exercise the muscles and joints of your hand. But many people claim even greater, more powerful results from these ancient, Oriental balls. For instance, some believe that our ten fingers connect with the cranial nerves and vital organs of the body. Plucking the balls with your fingers, therefore, may stimulate the key points on the hand and release vital energy. Users believe that these metal orbs can prevent and cure hypertension. People have been using these balls since the Ming Dynasty (1368-1644 AD).

Let's pretend: animals that turn into Balls

Some animals, like the opossum and the killdeer (a bird), play dead in the hopes that a predator will move on to a fresher meal. But some animals would rather play ball than play dead. When scared, startled, or under attack, these animals curl up into a ball to protect themselves.

ball python

Although it's got plenty of teeth, a powerful bite, and venom to boot, this snake defends itself from warthogs, leopards, and birds of prey by rolling into a ball and tucking its head into the center of itself.

pill bug

Also known as a roly poly, or *Armadillium vulgare* (if you like to speak Latin), these pearl-sized creatures are actually crustaceans, like crayfish, lobsters, and crabs. Pill bugs breathe through gills that require moisture, which explains why you usually find them under flowerpots and in other damp places. When they are disturbed, they roll up into little round balls.

pangolin

What looks like an anteater dressed up as an artichoke? The pangolin! This creature has a 16-inch-long tongue, a toothless mouth, and a tail that has more vertebrae than any other mammal. Like the pill bug, the pangolin rolls into a ball so its outer armor can protect its softer underbelly.

hedgehog

The more this little critter curls its body, the pricklier it becomes. The hedgehog has

about 5,000 spines that stick out, crisscrossing each other to make a tough shield. It has very loose skin and a powerful muscle around the edge of its "shell" that cinches tight, drawing the hedgehog's head and limbs inside.

armadillo

This ancient mammal (no relation to the hedgehog) has a tough *carapace* (outer shell) made of bony plates covered by horny skin. To protect itself, it draws in its head and limbs and curls into a tight ball. Some of its prehistoric ancestors grew to be ten feet long and weighed more than 220 pounds. South American natives made roofs for their homes from the armadillo's empty carapace.

I know, I know. You've reached the end of this book and you're wondering, "Where's the baseball? The bowling ball? The marbles, billiard balls, beach balls, and the rest of my favorite round things?" Fear not! Roll with it! You can only juggle so many balls at once, so another volume of *Balls!* is bouncing your way soon. Until then, this *Balls!* is in your court!

FOR FURTHER READING

SOME INTERESTING BOOKS AND WEB SITES TO BOUNCE AROUND

Sports and Balls in General

Chronicle of the Olympics. Updated edition. New York: Dorling Kindersley, 1998. A rich hardcover filled with facts and statistics for anyone watching the Olympics or just wondering about the many events included in this global competition.

The Diagram Group. *The Sports Fan's Ultimate Book of Sports Comparisons.* New York: St. Martin's Press, 1982. A great, graphic guide showing the abilities, records, and equipment of many sports.

Dorling Kindersley, publisher of The DK Superguide series. Each book is an easy-to-read, handsomely photographed encyclopedia of a given sport, including soccer, basketball, tennis, football, baseball, and plenty of games that don't involve a ball and may still be interesting (hmmm…).

Galahad Books, publisher of the How to Talk series. Each book contains definitions of "ball talk" with lively illustrations by Taylor Jones. The series includes *How to Talk Football* (by Arthur Pincus), *How to Talk Golf* (Dawson Taylor), *How to Talk Basketball* (Sam Goldaper and Arthur Pincus), and *How to Talk Tennis* (Peter Schwed).

Web Sites

www.exploratorium.edu/sports/index.html
A swell science site to bounce around.

www.guinnessworldrecords.com
The official site for the most, the fastest, the longest, and the best!

www.hickoksports.com
A great glossary of popular expressions used in each sport.

www.howstuffworks.com
The curious kid's answer to most questions about how things work.

www.inventors.about.com/library/inventors/blsports.htm
Who invented what—and how!

www.kidzworld.com/site/the_zone.htm
Kidz World has an online magazine about sports in the news.

www.refdesk.com/sports.html
A huge search tool with many links to official sports organizations and fact sheets.

www.sikids.com
The kids' version of *Sports Illustrated* magazine on the Web.

www.streetplay.com
A great collection of favorite, "less professional," neighborhood games, including boxball, stoopball, punchball, and dozens of others, with easy-to-follow explanations of each game.

www.usolympicteam.org
The site of the United States Olympic teams, with bios, statistics, photos, medals, and a special kids' section.

www.worldalmanacforkids.com/explore/sports.html
An online almanac with a section devoted to each major sport.

Other Sites and Such:

Almost every professional, collegiate, and Olympic team will have an official Web site. Try the team name with a ".com" or a ".org" after it, or use a search engine, such as Google, to find the site. In basketball and football, most teams have entire books devoted to their history, as well. Just "roll" into your local library.

Basketball

Lannin, Joanne. *A History of Basketball for Girls and Women*. New York: Lerner Sports, 2000. An overview of women in hoopland.

Mullen, Chris with Brian Coleman. *Basketball. DK Superguides*. New York: DK Publishing, Inc., 2000. A pictorial guide for kids all about the game, its rules, and plays.

Shoulder, Ken, et. al. *Total Basketball: The Ultimate Basketball Encyclopedia*. Toronto: SPORT Media Publications, 2003. At 1,470 pages, if there's something about basketball not in this book, it won't be on the quiz, so don't worry.

www.fiba.com
Basketball around the world—the Federation of International Basketball's official site.

www.hoophall.com
Site of the Basketball Hall of Fame.

www.nba.com
The National Basketball Association's official site.

www.ncaasports.com
The National College Athletic Association's official basketball site.

www.ncaabasketball.net/kidsCourt
Part of the NCAA's site devoted just to kids on the court.

www.scoutbb.com
An amazing page of links to nearly every "hoopful" thing on the planet.

www.spalding.com
Spalding, the maker of basketballs and other sports equipment.

Soccer

Hornby, Hugh, *Eyewitness Books: Soccer*. New York: DK. 2005.

Widdows, Richard. *The Arco Book of Soccer Techniques and Tactics*. New York: Arco Publishers, 1983. A solid guide to the basic plays of soccer.

www.fifa.com
The site of the international soccer governing body: the Fédération Internationale de Football Association.

www.footy4kids.co.uk
A great coaching site from the United Kingdom.

www.soccerballworld.com
Plenty of discussions and articles on the evolutions of the soccer ball and the game.

www.soccerhall.org
Website of the National Soccer Hall of Fame and Museum.

www.ussoccer.com
The United States Soccer Federation site.

Football

King, Peter. *Sports Illustrated Football: A History of the Professional Game*. Birmingham: Oxmoor House, 1993.

www.thehistoryoffootball.com
Just what it says! Your online history lesson.

www.nfl.com
The National Football League's official site.

www.playfootball.com
The NFL's kids' site.

www.profootballhof.com
The NFL's Hall of Fame site.

Tennis

Collins, Bud. *Total Tennis: The Ultimate Tennis Encyclopedia.* Toronto: Sport Classic Books, 2003. A giant volume, gathering most everything about the sport.

www.itftennis.com
The International Tennis Federation's official site.

www.pennracquet.com
Take a look at the manufacturing plant where tennis balls are hatched!

www.tennis.about.com
A great mix of tennis facts, records, and resources, hosted by tennis pro Jeff Cooper.

www.tennisfame.com
The International Tennis Hall of Fame's site.

Handball and Squash

www.usateamhandball.org
All about the game of team handball.

www.ushandball.org
The United States Handball Association's site.

www.us-squash.org
A site devoted to the game of squash in the United States.

Golf

Duno, Steve. *K-I-S-S Guide to Playing Golf.* New York: DK Publishing, 2000. A large paperback detailing all rules, terms, concepts, and details of the sport.

Peper, George, and the editors of *Golf Magazine. Golf in America.* New York: Harry N. Abrams, 1988. A picture survey of golfing in the United States.

Woods, Tiger. *How I Play Golf.* New York: Warner Books, 2001. Many photographs show how the legendary player practices, plots, and plays his game.

www.golfballmuseum.co.uk
An online museum dedicated to the history of the golf ball.

www.golfdigest.com
The famous golf magazine's online site.

www.juniorlinks.com
A golfing site devoted to kids' golfing, sponsored by several U.S. professional organizations.

www.kidzworld.com/site/p445.html
A special feature on Kidz World about the golf ball.

Volleyball

Lucus, Jeff. *Pass, Set, Crush.* Weratchee, Washington: Euclid Northwest Publishing, 1985. Sketches of all the basic moves and plays in volleyball.

www.volleyball.about.com
A guided tour of volleyball topics.

www.volleyball.org
General information on the sport.

Ping-Pong or Table Tennis

www.ittf.com
The official site of the International Table Tennis Federation.

www.pongworld.com
A general information site about table tennis (or Ping-Pong, if you prefer).

www.usatt.org
The U.S. Table Tennis official site, which has a special link to a "junior" page of table tennis fun and games.